Soccer Offense

Chest Dugger

Contents

Free Gift Included

As part of our dedication to help you succeed in your career, we have sent you a free soccer drills worksheet. This is the "Soccer Training Work Sheet" drill sheet. This is a list of drills that you can use to improve your game; as well as a methodology to track your performance on these drills on a day-to-day basis. We want to get you to the next level.

Click on the link below to get your free drills worksheet.

https://soccertrainingabiprod.gr8.com/

You can also get this book for free as an audiobook on Audible along with a free 1-month Audible membership. Just sign up for it using the link below:

https://www.audible.com/pd/B07G24HPWN/?source_code=AUD FPWS0223189MWT-BK-ACX0-123516&ref=acx_bty_BK_ACX0_123516_rh_us

ABOUT THE AUTHOR

Chest Dugger is a pen name for our soccer coaching team, Abiprod. Abiprod is a team of passionate professional coaches and fans, based in UK and Australia. You can check us out at www.abiprod.com

We have been fans of the beautiful game for decades, coaching junior and senior teams. Like every soccer fan around the globe, we watch and play the beautiful game as much as we can. Whether we're fans of Manchester United, Real Madrid, Arsenal or LA Galaxy; we share a common love for the beautiful game.

Though our experiences, we've noticed that there's very little information for the common soccer fan who wants to escalate his game to the next level. Or get their kids started on the way. This is especially the case for those who live outside Europe and South America. Expensive soccer coaching and methodology is pretty rare in even rich countries like USA and Australia.

Being passionate about the game, we want to get the message across as many people as possible. Through our soccer coaching blog, books and products; we aim to bring the best of soccer coaching to the world. Though we are starting off in USA and Australia, anyone who's passionate about the beautiful game can use our tactics and strategies.

DISCLAIMER

Introduction

Thank you for buying this book. Soccer is the most popular team sport in the world. It incites passion in players, pundits and supporters and leads to enormous loyalties to followers. It is the simplest of games, but one upon which tactical skills can be layered as we might find in the closest of chess matches.

But the aspect of soccer that lifts the crowds to their feet, gets them cheering and, usually, offers the greatest thrills to players and supporters alike is when a team attacks. The superb piece of individual skill, the piercing pass that splits a defence like a bread knife breaking a closely bound loaf, the shot, or header that screams into the net. That is what is at the heart of soccer.

And the game is definitely changing to see offensive philosophies overtake more defensive formations as the principals by which top teams orchestrate their play. From the great Arsenal sides of the late 1990s and early 2000s, under the tutelage of Arsene Wenger, through the development of tikka-taka play of the noughties' Barcelona team, through the high pressing, strong attacking style of the likes of Pep Guardiola, who of course started with the Spanish giants, and Jurgen Klopp, the best club sides have built their success on offensive play, trusting themselves to outscore the opposition in any given game.

And that has all been to the benefit of the fan, who see more goals – the tactical 0-0 or hope for a goal from a set piece to barely enliven a boring, safe soccer display are largely now removed to the closet of soccer's history.

This book will look at offensive plays. It will offer insight to coaches, players and supporters, young and old, and provide drills and analysis that can both help us to better understand the game and produce higher quality in attacking moves ourselves, or with our teams.

We hope that you find it interesting, and informative. And that it makes your team, your coaching or your own offensive play more effective.

Why Offensive Plays Are the Beating Heart of Soccer

Soccer is the most played team sport in the world. When three kids lay down their shirts on the grass of the park, and start a kick around, what do they play? A keeper and two to shoot, or cross or head the ball.

They play attacking football. Yes, the artistry of midfield – and we will return to this later – and the chess like tactics of defending are interesting in their own right, but what we want to see – whether fans or players or coaches – is exciting, goal scoring action.

Let us spend a while considering the greatest players of all time. Who might emerge in our list of top ten of all time? Well, Pele has to be there, of course. Probably the greatest exponent the game has ever seen. Maradona, for all his later troubles, possessed the kind of flair that set the field alight. From the modern game, Lionel Messi and Ronaldo probably deserve their place in this top ten, especially the former, who many feel is the only real rival to the great Brazilian mentioned above. The squat, powerful Hungarian Ferenc Puskas, star player of the Mighty Magyars makes the list and so do the elusive skills of George Best, a player who never graced the biggest stage of all. That German goal machine, Gerd Muller is difficult to leave off any list. Johan Cruyff, Dutch master of the mighty total football team of the 1970s is the eighth player. Perhaps the mercurial Michel Platini makes number nine on the list and the incredible Eusebio should appear as well. Some fans will add Zinedine Zidane in place of one of the above.

But let us consider some of the greats missed off that list. How many would find a place for the great liberoes Bobby Moore and Franz Beckenbauer, perhaps the finest defenders ever to grace the field. Or Lev Yashin, probably the best goalkeeper ever who saved no fewer than 150 penalties in his career.

The thing is, that first paragraph is full of great attackers, or attacking midfielders; the second is loaded with defensive players. Now we see the likes of Beckenbauer and Yashin, perhaps some of us would add them, but they are not the first players to come to mind (unless a love of defending is what motivates us in the game). No, soccer is about attackers, offensive players who make things happen. We can admire a great save, a superbly timed interception or perfectly placed positional play, but it is the screaming shot, the mazy dribble, the outrageous pass that brings us most often to our feet.

Further proof of the dominance of attacking play in our beautiful game can be seen when we consider the most expensive players of all time. Although it saddens many, soccer these days is big business at the highest levels, and the super-rich owners of clubs will not sanction major spending unless it will bring returns – either in trophies, crowd numbers or sales of merchandise. It is the offensive players who deliver these, and that is why they cost the most money.

Consider the following list:

1. Neymar Jr - from Barcelona to PSG in 2017 for $277 million; a striker.

2. Kylian Mbappe – from Monaco to PSG in 2018 for $234 million; an attacking midfielder

3. Phillipe Coutinho – from Liverpool to Barcelona in 2018 for $204 million: a Number 10.

4. Ousmane Dembele – from Borussia Dortmond to Barcelona in 2017 for $136 million; an attacking midfielder.

5. Paul Pogba – from Juventus to Manchester Utd in 2016 for $124 million; he would see himself as an attacking midfielder, although he is played (not very successfully, it could be argued) in a deeper role in a fairly defensively minded current Manchester United team.

6. Gareth Bale – from Spurs to Real Madrid in 2013 for $120 million; a wide attacker.

7. Cristiano Ronaldo – from Manchester Utd to Real Madrid in 2009 for $117 million; a striker

8. Gonzalo Higuain – from Napoli to Juventus in 2016 for $105.5 million; a striker

9. Luis Suarez – a striker from Liverpool to Barcelona in 2014, Romelu Lukaku, a striker from Everton to Manchester Utd for $105 million in 2017 and, finally, a defender makes this list. Virgil Van Dijk was bought from

Southampton by Liverpool in 2018. Each of these players cost $105 million.

10. The only other player to cost in excess of $100 million was Neymar Jr once more, when he first moved to Barcelona, from Santos, in 2013.

So, of the 12 most expensive players of all time, all but one is attack minded. If we continued the list to encompass the top twenty costliest footballers ever, we find a couple of attacking midfielders and the remainder are strikers. If we therefore accept that offensive play is what brings the crowd to the stadia, provides the biggest excitement in the game and is the main reason for participating in soccer, then we should look at the types of attacking plays that deliver this ultimate sporting thrill.

The Transition Stage

In the following chapters we look at set plays from attacking perspectives. We will consider corners, free kicks in direct shooting positions, free kicks from wide angles, attacking throw ins and penalties. We will look at the skills of offensive play that can lead to goals – dribbling, passing and shooting. Consideration will be given to formations, and how they can support offensive soccer and we will look at how passing moves can be developed to create opportunities. Indeed, we will attempt to cover all bases as we seek to demonstrate the secrets of attacking soccer.

But we will start by considering the circumstances in a game that most often leads to shots on goal, that is the transition from defending to attacking, and the way this can lead, for the best sides, to playing on the break. In other words, capitalizing on the point at which possession is won, and how the injection of speed and good decision making in this situation can exploit lack of defensive organization in teams who were themselves on the attack a moment before.

Around the time of writing this book, it was the Champions League last 16 in Europe. One match in particular typified how the transition phase is taking control of world football. The match was Barcelona versus Chelsea. The first leg in Spain had ended one a piece, which meant that the English club would need a high scoring draw or a win to progress. Barcelona are, of course, probably the best club side in the world at the moment; since most would argue that club soccer is now played at a higher elite level than international soccer, that possibly makes the Spanish outfit the best in the world.

Well, Chelsea were superb – their fans, the neutrals and even their detractors could not have failed to be impressed by the way they peppered the Barcelona goal with shots, hitting the woodwork twice. Barcelona, meanwhile, were on the back foot, chasing shadows and pinned in their own half. The final score? Barcelona 3 Chelsea 0. Never has such a score line failed to reflect the progress of a match.

And the reason for this one-sided result was that Chelsea made four mistakes, giving the ball away on each occasion when launching an attack. Barcelona scored from three of these errors, and on the fourth they still hit the target, with Courtois, Chelsea's Belgian 'keeper making a good save.

The first saw a rapid interchange of passes before the Uruguayan striker Luis Suarez put through Lionel Messi to score from an impossibly tight angle. The second saw Messi himself win the ball just inside his own half, and break at great speed, beating two defenders before pulling the ball back for Dembele to drive into the roof of the net. The third again saw Chelsea dispossessed in the Barcelona half, as they sought to launch yet another attack. The Spaniards drove forward with four players and a quick interchange of passes once again saw the great Argentinian, Messi, scoring low past the keeper.

Beyond that, it was all Chelsea.

But with such importance now associated with the transition – for our purposes in this book the one between defence and attack rather than the other way around – it is worth spending some time looking at the tactics of transition, and how teams can set up to maximize their offensive capabilities in such situations.

Turning Defence into Offense, the Theory

When a team wins the ball, it should look to exploit gaps in the opposing defensive lines which have come about because the opposition was attacking. It needs to work at speed, before the opposition can re-organize.

Stage One – Pitch Awareness

Players should be encouraged to develop their awareness of spaces on the pitch from an early age. This involves encouraging them to scan the field periodically. This will not only help them to perform their own defensive duties when not in possession but to identify lines of offense when they win back possession.

This will then help them to make their runs into spaces if they are not in possession, and to know where to pass if they are.

Drill: This skill is best taught in the game situation, especially small sided games. The coach gives regular instruction to 'Scan' as the game is played. After a time, it will become second nature to players to do this. At the end of sessions, some time should be spent during feedback to analyze the amount of times each player did scan the pitch. It should be every few seconds.

Identifying Transition Points

Good teams hunt in packs. Players know their roles in any given situation. When not in possession players should always be engaged in one of the following four duties:

1. Pressuring the player with the ball. This will usually be the closest player when the ball is received by the opposition.

2. Supporting the player putting on the pressure. This is important when the opposition are in a position to shoot or play a pass that will create a goal scoring opportunity. It will usually be the second closest player to the opposition player with the ball.

3. Marking a player. Some teams will set up with man to man marking, although as a concept this is becoming a little old fashioned.

4. Marking a space. Here, players identify and cover areas of the pitch into which opponents may make a run or pass. Covering a space might also include being the 'out' player to whom a pass will be played if transition occurs.

Drill: Play 5 v 5 or 6 v 6 on a large grid 30m by 20m. The aim is to keep possession. The coach encourages communication on the pitch as players instruct each other whether to pressure, cover etc. The coach may need to be the person doing this calling initially, but ultimately it is important that the team does so. When possession is lost, roles simply reverse, with the aim still to keep possession.

The skill develops by teams identifying likely transition points. These are usually one of the following:

- When a player receiving a pass has a poor first touch, and the ball runs away from him or her.

- When the player in possession struggles under pressure from an opponent, and the cover player also joins in to dispossess the opponent.

- When a pass is wayward, or difficult to control for a player under pressure, such as at head height or bobbling badly. A pass made under pressure is less likely to be accurate than one made when the passer is in plenty of space.

Drill: Still with our short-sided game, we introduce the concept of spotting a likely transition stage. When one of the above errors is identified, players need to know their jobs.

- The player making the tackle or interception will usually need an 'out pass' because they will not be in total control of the ball themselves. That 'out pass' needs to be shortish and played to a player in space.

- Attacking players need to make runs into the spaces they have identified through their regular scanning. These runs should be away from the receiver of the ball, giving that player space to dribble at speed or pass under no pressure.

- Team mates decide whether to support the attack or retain their shape. In an 11 v 11 game, four or five players should usually commit to the break, while others spot those who have made their runs, and ensure that they keep a solid defensive shape should transition change again. Once again, the London based Chelsea team featured in a good example of when this goes wrong recently. Playing in the FA Cup quarter final against Leicester City, they lost possession on the attack, and Leicester broke at speed. However, they committed too many players to their break, and when Chelsea won possession back once more, it required only two passes to leave a pacy striker one v one with the 'keeper, against whom he scored with ease.

- Playing 7 v 7 up to 11 v 11 the coach frequently stops the game to point out good and ineffective moves, focusing on each player doing their job when the transition occurs. Where necessary the transition can be artificially created as the coach stops the game and allocates possession to the other team. Play then continues from the position at which the game was stopped.

Drill: This time, a coach could start with 6 v 6 situations on the same sized pitch and once players have become adept at decision making, increase the numbers on each side to create a realistic match situation. However, the coach should also remember that the bigger the number of players on each team, the less individual opportunities their players will have to be actively involved in the drill, so more time should always be spent on the small sided drills.

The 6 v 6 drill now features a small goal at either end, but no goalkeeper. One team begins with possession and seeks to create a goal scoring opportunity against their organized opponents. If they succeed, possession simply changes. However, the purpose of the drill is to create opportunities for transition. When the play does break down, and transition occurs, it is important that every player knows their job. One player wins or intercepts the ball. Another moves into space to receive the pass. One to three more make runs. At least two retain good defensive positions (one might be the initial ball winner) should the attack break down.

A good coaching point is to sometimes stop the break before it fully develops. The coach blows their whistle, and everybody stands still. The coach is then able to help players analyze their positioning and their runs. Question to set would include:

- Have you found space?
- Are you creating space for the player in possession by drawing defenders away from their chosen positions?
- Is their either an easy pass for the player in possession, or has enough space been created for that player to dribble at speed?
- Has the team over or under committed players to the transition?
- What communication took place.

Another important coaching point it to encourage flexibility among the players. Yes, a striker is MORE LIKELY to join in the break, as are QUICKER PLAYERS and WING BACK who can create space from their naturally wide position. The best PASSER should, ideally, receive the 'out ball' since they are most likely to make the pass that will lead to a goal scoring opportunity. CENTRAL DEFENDERS are the least likely to join in the attack and are more likely to be the ones holding their positions should the transition phase reverse.

However, soccer is a fluid game, and the best teams make good decisions on the spot, seeking the best team outcomes from the position that they are in. Therefore, the coach could, in the drills, take players out of their normal positions to enable them to experience different roles.

Drill: While it is absolutely true that teams need to react to the situation when a transition occurs, there are 'normal' routes that can be practised. Normally, the out ball will look to be played to a fairly central position because from there the most options are available. Normally strikers will seek to angle a run wide to create space in the middle of the park. Often, full backs, wide midfielders or wing back will seek to break on the opposite wing to the one to which the striker moves in order to maximize passing opportunities and create the most challenge for the stretched defence.

Teams can practice this in unopposed situations. The drill begins with the ball going to the tackler, or interceptor, and players are placed in realistic positions for defence by the coach. They then practice standard moves, as outlined above, so that when such a situation lends itself on the field, players are drilled to make good runs.

Transition is a vital aspect of offensive play. Most teams are organized against normal attacks, and once they can get into a strong position of lines of 4-1-4 or 4-5 it is very hard to break them down. However, that organization is not there at the point of transition, as they themselves will have committed players out of position for their own attack.

Working on the transition is not just instinctive. While certain players are better than others at winning possession, making the decisive pass, getting forward in support and making runs, every player can improve themselves in these areas with regular drills and developed tactical awareness.

It is an aspect of the game that all coaches, and players, should familiarize themselves, and practice regularly if they are to maximize their offensive capabilities. This is true of them as individuals, but even more importantly for the contribution they can bring to the team as a whole.

Set Pieces

If the transition phase is the most common way to create a goal scoring opportunity, set plays can also be a strong offensive threat. They are of course the least fluid of soccer attacks, and that makes them the most coachable.

In this chapter we will look at a range of offensive set plays: corners, throw ins, the long throw, wide angle free kicks, attacking indirect free kicks, and free kicks that can lead to a direct shot on goal. We will also consider penalties. This chapter will include drills for all set plays, which the coach or player can used to maximize their team's potential in this important area.

Set Pieces – Some Background

Data analysis of set piece play demonstrates a number of results. None are terribly surprising. Teams identified as stronger score a lower percentage of their goals from set plays, perhaps because they look to get the ball moving quickly, rather than launching it into the box. However, those teams tend to be convert the highest percentage of their set plays into goals – perhaps because opponents are surprised when they do launch a direct attack, and also that they have players of better quality to deliver or finish effectively.

Often, teams with a higher percentage of total goals scored from set plays score less goals in total, suggesting that where it is possible to attack using alternative methods, then this is, overall, more successful.

It is also easier to defend set pieces than normal play, because teams can be drilled to protect their goal from these situations. However, at any level, set pieces are important. They create goal scoring opportunities, and if a side is weaker than its opponents, set plays can be a great leveler. It is certainly the case that time spent working on these plays is a good use of resources used in training sessions.

Corners

In fact, very few goals originate from corners. Statistics suggest that it the rate is just under one goal per seventy corners. That is about one goal every ten to twelve matches. However, corners are a regular feature of games, and that figure can be challenged by the data from the 2012/13 English Premier League, where just over a tenth of total goals scored originated from a corner.

The reason for the generally low rate is that accuracy of shots (including headers) from corners is far lower than in normal play. The reason for this is easy to work out. Because defences are drilled to defend from corners, attackers rarely have time or space to complete their goal attempt. Where shots are accurate it is much harder to place them away from the goalkeeper, and the extra number of bodies in the box compared to normal play means that there is a far greater chance that a shot will be deflected wide.

On top of that, most corners are cleared by defences, rather than reaching a striker. Nevertheless, enough goals are scored to make them worthwhile to practise. Short corners are generally more effective than long corners, as these lead to fewer players in the penalty area and offer crossing position from more advantageous starting points. Defensive formations are also less effective because the players in these have been drawn out of position.

Drill – Long Corners: Statistics demonstrate that there are three main areas from which goals are scored direct from corners. These are the near post, where the ball is flicked on; the far post, where the ball evades all defenders for an attacker arriving late, and around 6-10 yards out in the centre of the goal, often here goals are scored because of defensive errors or as the result of a second striker from a rebound or poor clearance.

Therefore, it makes sense to attack these areas. The best way to do this will depend on the defensive system used by opponents, and because often this will not be known before the game begins, it is worth working on attacks for both systems. The two defensive systems are zonal and man marking. A zonal system places defenders in the key areas of the penalty area, with players positioned to ensure that attackers do not get a shot in their area. Its strengths are that the best headers of the ball can be placed in the best positions, and there should not be space in the key 'scoring' zones. The disadvantage is that defending is static, and attackers running into the space may get an extra leap on their defender since they are coming from a moving start. The alternative, man marking system has the advantage that it should prevent any attacker from getting a shot or header on the ball. It falls down when something goes wrong, and an attacker is missed. This means that the offensive side can get free shots from dangerous positions. Statistically, the zonal system has proved to be slightly more successful.

In either case, attacking drills should seek to put players in the following positions:

- Near post
- Centre of the goal
- Far post
- One to 'mark' the keeper
- One to come for a short corner, usually from the nearest corner of the box
- Two to be out for rebounds or pulled back corners
- Two to remain in defensive positions in case the corner goes wrong.

Each player needs to time their run. Normally, the three looking to run into space for a header will start as a group, each knowing where he is heading. The players seek to time their run so that a near post flick will be achieved before the near post defender can clear. The far post runner delays their run, seeking to arrive late and therefore unmarked. The central striker should not get too close to the goal line, as they will need to react to whatever happens as the corner is taken. The goalkeeper marker should seek to remain in front of the keeper, without fouling them, and move slightly off the goal line to ensure that they do not fall offside. The 'shooters' should look to stay on the edge of the box. Against zonal marking, making the runs is easier, but against man markers, the three runners can be shielded by the two 'shooters' to make it harder to mark. The runners should vary their runs, perhaps taking a step one way before accelerating the other, to help lose their markers.

Whether or not it is a short corner, players should make their runs, repositioning if a short corner is played.

The corner taker is key to the success of the attacking set piece. This should be the best hitter of a dead ball. Generally, with a long corner, the target is the near post player so that these can flick the ball on, something very difficult to defend against. Therefore, the corner taker should spend time working, unopposed, with his three 'runners', especially the near post man, so that timing can be perfected.

In swingers And Out swingers

There are two forms of long corner. The in swinger and out swinger. Generally, the out swinger is more effective. It is more likely to take the keeper out of their clearing role, as the ball will be too far away from the goal for them to collect. A right footed player taking a corner from their right-hand corner flag will produce an out swinger, a left footed player an in swinger.

Both forms should be practiced to make it harder for defenders.

Short Corners

The aim here is to create a 'spare player' so that a cross can be delivered from a different angle.

Drill: One player is by the corner flag, he should ideally be a player who can naturally deliver an in-swinging corner from his or her side since the wider angle for the cross now makes this a more effective offensive weapon. His partner starts on the corner of the penalty box. This player sprints towards the ball. The corner taker passes low at 45 degrees to this player. The corner taker immediately sprints behind his partner. This has now created a 2 v 1 in the attacking situation, and a second defender will need to come to close down the ball. The receiver has a choice, if there is time, he drives towards the goal and crosses. More likely, he passes first time behind him to the corner taker, who now delivers an in swinger from a wider angle.

Drill: Shooters: Shooters line up on the edge of the box. The coach feeds a variety of balls to them, some along the ground, some fast, some bouncing, some high. The coach is recreating the situation of what might happen in the game. Rarely is there time for two touches, a good defence never offers time for three.

The shooters work on two skills. First or second touch shooting. Volley passing wide to the corner taker (who has moved from the touchline towards the corner of the box) for just such a scenario.

It is essential that the shooters do not lose possession. An attacking corner can leave a side vulnerable to an attack on the break, as most of the team have gone forwards. Therefore, any ball that breaks must be passed wide immediately, to keep the attack going but also limit danger. Or it must result in a shot because in that situation, even if no goal is scored, the ball is likely to go out of play and allow the attacking side to re-organize defensively.

The shooters should practise shooting low, because with so many bodies in a box from a corner, there is a good chance of a deflection towards the goal.

Direct Shot Free Kicks

Around a third of total goals scored in football result from set plays and the biggest percentage of these come from direct free kicks. However, they are still relatively rare with most professional specialists only scoring one or two a season. There are exceptions; in the first three month of the 2015/16 season the Brazilian Willian took shots from eleven free kicks. He hit the post one, had three saved and scored six of his attempts.

It is possible to analyze the best positions for taking a shot from a free kick, and also the best types of kick to perform. We can then get our players to practise this and identify the best takers from various positions to utilize the best outcomes for the side.

Drill: Our players can practise the type of direct free kick that is most successful in terms of returning goals. This is a curve shot. The skill is to strike the ball with the inside of the foot, near the toes rather than instep to ensure power.

The run up should be from wide, and the kicking foot strikes through the ball. The follow through is full and ends with the foot high. This imparts both side spin, the make the ball curve, and top spin to make the ball drop. With these elements the ball can be hit away from the keeper but will come back to end up inside the post, or with an opposite direction, will move away from keeper and find the other corner. The top spin element will allow the ball to clear the wall but still drop enough to enter the goal.

Free kicks are difficult to score, and require precision, power, technique and accuracy. However, with practice players will become more adept at delivering them on target.

Although shots with the instep are more accurate, usually insufficient power is delivered to beat a goalkeeper. The ball needs to end up in a corner, ideally the top corner, but some success is gained with shots low down in the corner. Mid height shots, or those that end up in a central part of the goal, are usually saved.

Goals are most often scored from free kicks taken in line with the D of the penalty area, and those from a distance of 27 metres are the most likely of these to end in the net. This distance is close enough for the power or the shot to still be troublesome to a goalkeeper, and far enough out for the ball to clear the wall and come down to goal height afterwards.

An in swinging shot is also worth trying from areas in line with the edge of the box but from a position between the corner and the touchline, as this is the second most successful position for goals to come about. However, in this situation a different kind of kick should be delivered. The most successful here are those that bounce in the centre of the goal and about 6 to 8 metres out. These types of freekicks often end up in the far corner. This is because attackers (and defenders) will be running on to the ball to shoot or clear. This means that goalkeepers have to leave their dive until late in case another player (under this sort of pressure, one from either side can result in a goal wards shot or deflection) makes contact. A free kick bouncing and curling into the far corner from this position can often beat a goalkeeper because their late dive means that they simply cannot reach the ball.

Drill: The drill for this is similar to that for the more central shot. Although the ball should still be struck firmly, it is the bounce rather than the power that will beat the goalkeeper here, so more instep can be used. There is usually a smaller wall to avoid. The drill can include attackers (and defenders) running in to try to get a touch.

Free Kick Assists

Here, we are talking about free kicks delivered into the box for strikers to head or shoot into the goal. This is the most common form of headed goal scoring assist from set pieces, out performing corners comfortably. Unsurprisingly, the highest ration of goals from free kicks come when the free kicks are between the edge of the penalty area and about a third of the way back to the half way line. In swinging corners account for the majority of goals scored.

This kind of free kick presents great difficulty for defences. They will line up as far up as possible to give the goalkeeper as much chance of claiming the ball as possible as this is the best defence against these kicks, but this creates the problem of a well-directed kick entering an open region of the pitch, where a well-timed run might end in a free header. Most goals are scored from the centre of the goal area from these free kicks.

Drill: Bearing in mind the above, teams should practice delivering balls with swing and pace into the penalty area, as close to goal as possible but where the keeper cannot easily come and claim. That is an area around 8 metres from the goal line, depending on from how far the kick is coming. The further out, the more time the keeper has to reach the ball, so the shorter the cross must be.

The drill will develop by adding runners to get on the end of the crosses. Finally, defence should be added, with the attackers lining up in a way that protects a run, for example, in a group of three where one will make the run, and the other two ensure that man marking is difficult.

Another tactic that can be practised is to have a striker or two standing in an offside position before the ball is struck. This player or players then moves onside – i.e. away from the goal – as the ball is struck, distracting defenders away from the targets making runs to the mid and far post regions.

Teams should drill from both sides, using a left and right footed player if at all possible.

Statistically, when the ball is more than twenty-five metres from the touch line, or closer than twelve, few goals are scored. In this situation, players should look to take a quick free kick, with the aim of utilizing space before a defense has become organized.

Throw Ins

Few goals are scored as a result of a throw in. Generally speaking, it is best to look for a quick throw before a team can get organized defensively, and play the ball in with a cross, or a pass cross-field for a midfielder to run onto. However, sometimes a team will have a specialist long thrower, and this can become a big threat for defences.

Such throws should be aimed in a similar place always, so that they can be practised. A tall striker should be the target. Defences, usually including the keeper, will attempt to win the ball. The hope, from an attacking perspective, is that the second ball will fall to an attacker for a simple finish.

Long throws are most effective if they are flat and fast. With the aim for an attacking or defensive flick on, they are best aimed for the near post. The intention is to be close enough to the keeper to tempt them to come.

Drill: Where a team possesses a player with a long throw, the team should work on throwing accurately to a region, the target getting a flick on and two or three runners gambling on the location of the flick. Initially, for accuracy, the drill can be practised unopposed, although later defence should be added to make the situation closer to a match day scenario.

Penalties

Penalties contain the fewest variables and can therefore be analyzed and best practice identified. Players can then practice them. However, there is one factor with penalty taking that is hand to work on, and that is the pressure of the situation for the taker. A penalty is the only occasion in a game where a striker is expected to score. Even a one on one with a keeper leaves the striker in a position where a goal is no more than a fifty-fifty outcome, but from a penalty, there is a strong expectation of scoring.

Replicating that kind of pressure in drills is not possible. However, for all of this, we do know that working on any skill in soccer will help it improve.

We do know that there are four areas of the goal where the keeper will not be able to stop the shot, these being the top and bottom corners on either side of the goal. However, the margin for error of these is the narrowest, and with a pressure situation it is possible to mis-direct a penalty to these areas.

Hitting the ball straight is a good method as well. Keepers will nearly always commit themselves one way or the other, so a shot down the middle, particular one lifted, gives a wide margin for error.

Strikers also sometimes try to disguise their timing with a pause in a run up to get the keeper to commit early – they will then direct their kick to the other side. It is certainly worth having two or three regular penalty takers, who work on the skill in training. However, ultimately it is down to the personality type to know which players will take penalties without fear, knowing that if they miss they will be able to bounce back. It is the skill of the coach to identify this attribute in his team.

Open Play Offensive Tactics – Creating Space As A Team

We have looked at the two situations where a team's offensive play might exploit a weakness in defence; that is on the break following the transition stage and from set piece moves.

The third element for offensive play is during the normal course of a match. Here, when a defensive line up is in place, it is the tricks and skills of the team and individuals that can create the goal scoring opportunity. And of course, it is on the training ground where coaches can work on such moves to maximise their team's offensive opportunities.

Team Plays: Creating Space for A Cross

We can see quite quickly when we look at team plays how they are largely about getting an extra player in an attacking situation to create space for a top-quality pass, cross of shot. Therefore, we can see as well that in doing this, a team is vulnerable to the break if the control of the ball transitions to the other team.

To some extent, this is unavoidable, but the best teams seek to ensure that their attacks end in a shot; even if it is off target, the fact that the ball will go out of play gives them time to re-organise as possession changes.

Of course, this is not always possible, and attacks sometimes break down before the point that a shot can be made; this is the joy of the game, and the best exponents are demonstrating that through attacking play, they will ultimately score more than they concede, and so become more successful as a team.

One of the best ways to create a shooting (or heading) opportunity is to create space for a cross into the penalty area.

There are two main positions for crossing. The first, more traditional approach is for a player to get to the by line and pull the ball back and into the penalty area. This might be in the air or, if the positions of the defence allow, pulled back along the ground.

The second crossing position is developing more in the modern game, and that is the cross from deep. We will look at this shortly but begin with the cross from the by line.

There are drills that can be practised to gain success in achieving these crosses. One method is about individual skills, which we will consider in the next chapter, but here we provide a drill for creating an overlap and thus allowing a cross to be delivered.

Drill: The coach sets up cones to represent defenders. There are eight, in two banks of four spread across the pitch, one set on the edge of the area, the other approximately 8-10 metres further up the pitch. There are three attacking players in the drill.

Player One starts in the centre of the pitch on the half way line circle, in the attacking half. Player Two starts midway between the edge of the D and the touchline, on the half way line. Player Three is the full back or wing back and begins on the touchlines five metres inside his or her own half.

Two feeds the ball into One and breaks forward. Three breaks forward from wide. One dribbles the ball and feeds into Two between the banks of defenders. Two passes the ball through the final line of defenders wide into the path of Three. One and Two continue their run into the box. Three crosses – high or low. One or Two get on the end of the cross to score.

Coaching points:

- Three needs to sprint onto the ball to inject necessary pace into the attack

- Two's pass to three needs to be first time, again to inject pace.

- Three's cross needs to be away from where the keeper would be.

- When in the box, One and Two need the change the direction of their runs so that any defender tracking them will find it hard to stay close to them. That small amount of space created is what will give the opportunity to get a shot on target.

The drill can develop into an attack v defence session, starting 6 v 6 plus a goalkeeper. Here, the defence line up in two rows of three.

The spare attackers are there to make runs to draw defenders away (see the 'Making Runs' section later in the chapter) and create space for Two to get between the lines of defence to deliver the killer pass that leads to the cross and, hopefully, goal.

The second form of cross is the deeper cross, delivered from wide, but between 12 and 30 metres back from the touch line. This kind of cross is really like a free kick. There are plusses and minuses for taking this approach. On the positive side, often that is a part of the pitch where there is space for a good quality delivery to take place. Although few goals come about from the cross itself – usually the ball will be cut out, or the attacker will be under too much pressure to get a powerful header or shot in themselves, the next phase can create goal scoring opportunities. Defences are pushed back creating space between them and the next line of defensive midfielders. In that space, a skilful midfielder can pick up a poor clearance with the room to deliver a killer pass. The ball sometimes bobbles around after a cross of this kind, leading to shooting opportunities for the offensive team.

However, on the other hand possession is more likely to be given away. Logically, any cross cleared has a more than 50/50 chance of ending up with the opposition, since they will have both a goalkeeper who can collect the ball, and more players in the zone.

Nevertheless, we are seeing more and more of this kind of delivery happening in the modern game. Top coaches base their team plays on analytics, which indicates that overall this kind of deep cross must deliver results, and as such it is well worth including in any offensive play arsenal.

Drill: The secret to the deep cross lies in the delivery. Players can practise this easily. Firstly, the drill involves just three players. Player One starts with the ball and lays it off with a short pass into the crossing range (see above) to Player Two. Player Two takes one touch to shift the ball to a position where they can cross with their second touch. They deliver the cross, aiming for it to be at head height as it passes the penalty spot, or just behind. Player One makes a run towards the edge of the penalty area to pick up any loose clearances.

Player Three acts a goalkeeper to return the ball. The drill develops by adding firstly a striker, then two defenders then a second attacker and a third defender. Ultimately, it can be carried out in a full attack v defence session. The quality of the cross is all, with the second most important element being the support play to pick up rebounds.

Team Plays: The Switch In Play

The challenge for offensive plays when a team is set up defensively is to create the space to deliver the killer pass. When teams are organised, it is very difficult to find space, and under pressure even the best players are more likely to misplace a key pass than make it count. The answer is to find space for the killer assist – either one that leads directly to a goal scoring chance or creates the opportunity for a cross.

One way of achieving this is with the switch in play. This sees the ball cross the field in one or two passes (a maximum of three is possible provided the passes are sharp). The aim is to stretch the defence by moving it from side to side, eventually creating space between the two lines of defence for an attacking midfielder to exploit with a killer pass or assist.

The switch takes place in front of the further defensive line, taking care that any lingering attacker is unable to intercept. It requires the back four, and perhaps a deep lying midfielder, to be good passers and have a good touch on receipt of the ball.

The switch happens from side to side until the defence are shifted out of position. This is also a good long-term tactic, as it means that defenders and the lone attacker have to do a lot of running to keep their shape, while the team in possession do much less. Over the course of the game, this difference in running should lead to more spaces opening up for the attacking side as the defending team tire.

Drills: In terms of drills, the key skills are passing and first touch, and these are the ones that need to be practised. Simple passing in threes, switching from side to side, using one touch to control and the second to pass firmly will help to develop the confidence and technique in players to use to switch in play. The key coaching points are as follows:

- Strike the ball firmly with the instep, non-kicking foot firmly planted to the side, weight over the ball.

- Receiver moves body to get in line and receives on the full (they are not under pressure and so do not need to receive the ball on the half turn); their first touch takes the ball half a metre to the side, allowing them to pass with their next touch

Team Plays: Getting A Midfielder Beyond The Striker

Making the opportunities to score requires, against a well organised defence, the ability to provide an injection of pace, and to get extra players in goal scoring positions.

Some players are better at doing this than others, having a clearer 'picture' of what is happening around them, and thus innately knowing when to make their runs into the box. We are looking in this sub-section at the runs made by midfielders (or defenders, acting as midfielders) into goal scoring positions in anticipation of a through pass by a team mate, or a lay off from a striker.

There are two great benefits of midfielders making runs beyond their strikers, provided they get their timing right and remain onside. Firstly, such runs are far harder to track for defences. The defensive player providing the cover to track this kind of run is often not a full out defender, and therefore is likely to be less good at spotting the runs and covering them. When a member of the last line of defence is forced to follow the run, this creates space for other players.

Drills: As with many tactical drills, this skill is best worked on initially with a static defence, made of cones, to which real players are added later once the timing and skills have been ingrained into the relevant players. To make the situation more realistic, a goalkeeper can be added from the outset.

A good drill involves five players, four attackers and the goalkeeper. The coach sets up to blocks of four cones to represent the defence as in the drill earlier in this chapter.

Player One is the midfielder making the run.

Player Two is the midfielder making the assist pass

Player Three is the striker

Player Four is the space maker.

Player Five is the goalkeeper.

Player Two starts with the ball. Player Three comes short for a pass. Player Three will either lay the ball back to Player Two to make the assist or will flick the ball beyond the defence himself. Player four makes a diagonal run across the direction of play. The aim here is take a defender out of position and thus create the space for Player One to run into. Player One times his or her run to be level with the last defender at the time of the through pass, either by the midfielder of the striker. He or she should then run onto this pass and shoot past the goalkeeper.

Team Plays: The Late Run

In some ways similar to the run beyond the striker, a late run is one made by a midfielder to arrive at the far post, or edge of the box, when the ball is wide. The strength of a late run is that it is hard to cover for defences because they have been pulled out of position by the shifting of the ball wide.

The person making the late run is aiming to get on one of the following balls:

- One pulled back for them consciously by the crosser, while other strikers head to the near post, taking their defenders with them.
- To pick up balls that are missed by the attackers and defenders
- To pick up rebounds and deflections.

Drills: The same drills as for the crossing from the by line can be effective in working on this team play. However, the late running midfielder is added. This player either heads on an angled run to the far post, while the other attackers head for the near post or pulls their run to the edge of the box.

The key skills for the player making the late run are:

- Anticipation – that hard to define ability to see the picture unfolding before them

• A willingness to gamble on the ball ending up where they make their run. Usually it will not, which means the run has been wasted. Resilience towards this is therefore very important.

• The ability to score with both feet – the ball will come quickly, and often the situation is messy with lots of players diving in. There is rarely much chance for composure

• Bravery – often the player arriving late on the far post will need to throw their head towards a cross, or dive in to deflect the ball home.

• An accurate shot from the edge of the box. This will often be first time, and therefore good technique and body position are important.

Team Plays: The One/Two

As we have seen, in order to create opportunities for goals in open play situations, an injection of pace into an attack is a crucial attribute. One way of doing this is to use first touch passing, including the difficult to defend against one/two.

This move involves a player feeding a pass into a team mate and received a first touch pass in return. The player is moving forward and into space, and the speed of the lay off pass means that space is created. This kind of attack, when successful around the box, will often create a goal scoring opportunity. Another bonus is that out of position defenders will frequently commit fouls leading to set piece shooting opportunities.

Drill: As with many other drills, these skills can be build up slowly. A good starting point is a 10 x 10 metre grid and five players. One player is in the centre of the grid, and the others on the four outside lines.

The player in the centre passes to a team mate on the outside of the square, who hits a first-time return. The central player then lays off to another team mate. Speed and weight of pass all improve with practice, and players become more adept and confident with first time passing. The central player gets used to getting their body position right to receive and protect the ball, and also to lay it off to a different team mate.

The drill can develop firstly by adding one defender to pressure the central player.

Next, it can be played on a pitch with three players and the same defensive cones as in many of the drills listed above. There is a feeder, a receiver and a goalkeeper. The feeder lays the ball into the receiver, who protects the ball and lays it off first time, by receiving it on the half turn. The feeder picks up the return and shoots.

Body position is crucial here since the receiver will be under pressure. They should have their shoulder towards the ball so that they are half turned with a low centre of gravity and arms out for support.

The drill is developed further with the addition of a defender on the pitch.

The one/two can be developed into whole team first or second touch passing moves. Here, the ball moves quickly pressuring defenders and pulling them out of position. Such team plays can be worked on in training with five a side games, and one touch or two touch possession games.

Team Plays: Creating Space For The Killer Pass – Running Off The Ball

Soccer is a team game, and some of the best players, and easiest to have on a team, are the unselfish players prepared to make runs off the ball to create space for their colleagues.

These runs can draw defenders out of position, allowing a dribbler to continue their run, or make the space for a pass.

This skill is best developed through small sided games. *Drill:* A good starting point is a 4 x 4 game, where the aim is to keep possession, in a small 20 x 20 metre grid. In order to keep possession, the team will need to run off the ball to create space.

Coaching points:

- The coach should encourage communication. One of the keys of running off the ball is that a defender should know it is happening. That way the defence will track the runs, creating the space required.

- Good coaches will stop sessions often, pointing out effective runs, and those that add little to the offensive team

- Players should be encouraged to pass and move continuously. This involves a good first touch which both protects the ball and allows for a quick return pass.

In the match situation, running off the ball allows the player in possession to have time and options for passing or running with the ball.

Team Plays: The High Press

If we take ourselves back to the second chapter of this book, we looked at the importance of transition. One way to achieve the transition is also a kind of offensive play, and that is the high press.

Here, a team works together to put pressure on a defence as it seeks to play out and launch its own attack. Many successful teams work hard on the high press. It requires good teamwork, communication and excellent levels of physical and mental fitness, since a lot of running is required. It is therefore important to establish those fitness levels in training sessions.

The high press is a particularly useful team play for the offense because when it is successful, it means that players are already in a position to support an attack after the transition of possession.

This manoeuvre works by the team putting pressure on the player with the ball, right from the goalkeeper if possible, and team mates closing down opponents so that it becomes increasingly hard to find an easy pass for the side in possession.

Gradually, the opponents have less and less time on the ball, and therefore their own passing is pressured. That means that it is likely to become less accurate. That, in turn, puts pressure on the receiver to control what might be a poor pass when they, themselves, are quickly under pressure. Eventually, when the high press works well, teams lose possession either through an interception or a tackle. The transition then proceeds at pace, as in the examples in the earlier chapter, but also with increasing effect because players are already in attacking positions on the park, having been there to undertake their own pressuring.

Drills: A good way to start is to play a 3 v 2 possession game in a small, 10 x 10 metre square. For this, each side has two players, while the fifth player wears an identifying bib, and always plays on the side in possession. The team without the ball seek to close down opponents pressuring them into mistakes. When the ball leaves the grid, or an interception or tackle is made, possession changes and the bibbed player joins the other side.

This drill can then increase in every larger grid to 4 v 3, 5 v 4 etc, before turning into full scale match practice.

The key skills for the coach are:

- Ensure communication so that all players understand their job.

- Ensure the team closes down the opposition applying pressure. The tackle should only be attempted when an individual's ball control is lost. So, patience is a virtue to enhance.

- It is acceptable to force the team in possession into playing a long punt as that will usually mean a transfer of possession. What is not acceptable is for an easy out pass to become available because a player does not close down his opponent, or over commits on the pressure. That would mean the hard work of team mates is wasted.

Individual Skills

The final element to offensive play are the individual skills of a player in dribbling, passing and shooting that can create offensive opportunities. These skills can be developed in training and applied in matches.

Some players do, of course, have more skill in these areas than others, but good training will make all players comfortable on the ball, and therefore more likely to add to the offensive elements of a match.

Individual skills that can be worked on in training include:

• Running at pace, using the laces to ensure the ball is moved without breaking stride

• Dribbling skills including the change of direction, step over, turn (such as the Cruyff turn) and shuffle.

• Passing skills such as floated passes, backspin passes, passes with the inside and outside of the foot and both the short and long pass. First time passing is, as we saw above, a vital skill.

• Shooting skills such as driving with the laces, chipping, side foot 'passing the ball into the net' and headers – these should be downwards, power generated by strong neck muscles, or flick ones.

Team Formations

The formation of a team can also give a clue to its attacking intent. Playing five at the back is actually quite attacking, as it gives greater opportunity for the wing backs to get forward and support offensive plays. Playing two holding players in midfield, such as in 4, 2, 3, 1 takes some of the defensive duties away from the three attacking midfielders and gives greater securing with the ball is lost during an attack. The best teams will be fluid in their formation, shifting from, for example, 4, 5, 1 when defending, to 5, 2, 3 when moving forward.

Conclusion

I hope that you found this book on Offensive Plays in Soccer useful, and that there are ideas and drills that you can adapt to your own team or play. We have learned in this book about the importance of transition in offensive play. We have discovered the best ways to carry out set piece moves and we have analyzed many of the tricks and tactics that create goal scoring opportunities in open play.

Attacking or offensive play is at the heart of the beautiful game, and it is the element of the sport that should be encouraged most. Current trends are showing that even at the highest professional level, coaches are learning that attacking play will more often than not win out over negative tactics.

That is to the benefit of all. Most players, even defenders, love to attack; coaches like to see it and spectators love the elements of a game that lifts them to their feet – the dribble, the shot, the incisive pass, the goal.

Long may it continue.

CPSIA information can be obtained
at www.ICGtesting.com
Printed in the USA
LVHW080956201220
674416LV00013BA/1397